6·18·99

W9-CHN-527

THE GREAT WHEEL

ALSO BY PAUL MARIANI

POETRY

Timing Devices (1979)

Crossing Cocytus (1982)

Prime Mover (1985)

Salvage Operations:
New & Selected Poems (1990)

BIOGRAPHY

William Carlos Williams: A New World Naked (1981)

Dream Song: The Life of John Berryman (1990)

Lost Puritan: A Life of Robert Lowell (1994)

CRITICISM

A Commentary on the Complete Poems
of Gerard Manley Hopkins (1970)

William Carlos Williams:
The Poet and His Critics (1975)

A Usable Past: Essays on Modern
and Contemporary Poetry (1984)

THE
GREAT
WHEEL

PAUL MARIANI

W. W. NORTON & COMPANY

NEW YORK • LONDON

Some of these poems have appeared in the following periodicals and anthologies, to whose editors grateful acknowledgment is here made:
America, Boston Review, The Gettysburg Review, Image, The New Criterion, The New England Review, Poems for a Small Planet, Poetry, Quarterly West, River City, Sewanee Theological Review, Spiritual Life.

Lines from the final Canto of the "Paradiso" from *The Divine Comedy* translated by Allen Mandelbaum which appear in "Antiphon" are reprinted with the permission of Allen Mandelbaum and W. W. Norton & Company, Inc.

Lines from *The New Jerusalem Bible.* Copyright © 1985 by Doubleday, a division of Bantam Doubleday Dell Publishing Group, Inc. and Darton, Longman & Todd, Ltd. Used by permission of Doubleday, a division of Bantam Doubleday Dell Publishing Group, Inc.

Lines from William Carlos Williams, *Collected Poems 1939–1962, Vol. II.* Copyright © 1944, 1948, 1962 by William Carlos Williams. Reprinted by permission of New Directions Publishing Corporation.

For information about permission to reproduce selections from this book, write to Permissions, W. W. Norton & Company, Inc., 500 Fifth Avenue, New York, NY 10110.

The text of this book is composed in Palatino
with the display set in Bernhard Modern
Composition by PennSet, Inc.
Manufacturing by Courier Companies, Inc.
Book design by Jam Design

Library of Congress Cataloging-in-Publication Data

Mariani, Paul L.
    The great wheel / by Paul Mariani.
      p.   cm.
    ISBN 0-393-03921-8
    I. Title.
    PS3563.A6543G74   1996
    811'.54—dc20   95-37927

W. W. Norton & Company, Inc., 500 Fifth Avenue, New York, N.Y. 10110
W. W. Norton & Company Ltd., 10 Coptic Street, London WC1A 1PU

1 2 3 4 5 6 7 8 9 0

for Phil Levine
& for Bob Pack,
two who made the difference

CONTENTS

I

II

III

IV

Roll through my chant with all thy lawless music, thy
 swinging lamps at night,
Thy madly-whistled laughter, echoing, rumbling like an
 earth-quake, rousing all,
Law of thyself complete, thine own track firmly holding . . .
 WALT WHITMAN, "To a Locomotive in Winter"

It is as if the blissful agony or stress of selving in God had forced out
drops of sweat or blood, which drops were the world.
 GERARD MANLEY HOPKINS, 8 November 1881
 Meditation note on the Creation

 The business of love is
 cruelty which,

by our wills,
 we transform
 to live together.
 WILLIAM CARLOS WILLIAMS, "The Ivy Crown"

I

SHADOW PORTRAIT

In the ruined portrait by Siqueiros,
the face lifts like a death's head
from the shadows. White hair & blotched,
disfigured skin. The bruised lips
puffed & bleeding, *ecce homo*,

eyes sewn shut as if beseeching.
It is only 32, this face,
but like Villon's it knows, in spite of
whatever myths he feeds it, it cannot last
another year. Hiss of scorpions on the sands

at nightfall, hiss of seabeached turtles,
the waves advancing and retreating.
He strains to hear it all, as if somehow
he might fathom. It is not, he sees,
that what he looks at hard looks hard

back at him. Things hide themselves,
hold, then spit their hissing sibilants
back into his face. . . . Bougainvillea
& the banyan tree, palms aflame
with the firefeathered forms of avocets,

the bronze bells of Easter morning blooming.
Was this then the ecstasy of vision? This
and the boy he had there on the cobbled stones
of Taxco? Then self-exile, the phosphor waters
north of Cuba, the whirr of circling fins.

Beneath his fastened lids he watches
as the brilliance of the billowing sails
fails with night to return to empty sheets
of paper. He knows now that, wherever he is
going, there is no way he can make it.

STEPS

A cold wind rising on the creaking steps
    behind me: hard oak treads & risers varnished
        & revarnished these past hundred years,

built by some broken carpenter, ex-Union Army,
    in the employ of Alvah Clapp, who raised this house
        for his wife & daughters step by step

from the ashes of the fire that wiped out half
    the homes along this street. Ash long ago themselves.
        A hundred years, and again the chop-chop

quarternotes of children climbing to the reaches
    of the second floor, this time sons. The assured
        clump downstairs all but unassisted by their mother.

Prom strut, wheelabout, bounce and glide. The desultory
    halfnote pause, the scherzo footwork on the landing.
        Gone now: one to the distant province of Sonora,

my young Jesuit, learning how to bury the village dead
    in his less-than-steady Spanish. One intent on
        carving out the Great American Novel as he works

to keep his necessary half step ahead of forty lynx-eyed
    students. And the youngest, head bent beneath a bare
        lamp somewhere in the Bronx, Freud become his second

Moses. Gone now, step by step, and you know their mother
    knows it: the heft & creaking weight, the rise
        and sigh of each lovely ghost son's footfall.

Montague, Massachusetts

FALLING ASLEEP

Somewhere far from this room
there's a war going on, a war
where people fall down forever,
though he knows he is safe at least
here with his father, who is
lying beside him, his strong arm

nestled above him, trying
to get his young son to sleep.
Soon, his father has told him,
he will have to march off,
shouldering his duffle, his mother,
once again pregnant, stroking

the cropped head of his frightened
small brother. But here, here
in this room, the shadows wheeling
slowly about him, his father is still here
beside him, still breathing strongly
as the boy strains after the voices

somewhere below—his aunt & his uncle,
his nana, his mother—the sounds finding
their way up the steps, mixed with
the scents of polenta & chicken.
His father knows he would like
to stay up with the Big Ones,

though he *is* trying to sleep
just as fast as he can. Still, he knows
what he knows: that when he awakes
his father will have risen and left,
and one day his nana and one day
his aunt and his uncle and, yes,

one day even his mother. Again
and again he will wake to another one
gone, though for now, here in Astoria,
the four walls of the room with the cross
at one end and the early spring light
there for as long as the telling,

his father still lies beside him,
no emphysema yet, nor rasp to his
breathing, still blackmaned & strong,
as he winks at his son—man to man
says his father—to say now it's all
right and that now they can sleep.

VARIATIONS ON A THEME

Miami sunlight, as in a painting
by the poet Donald Justice:
a V of three pelicans drifting south
past the condos and the royal palms,
aflame now with the green scent
of coconut & parrot. Out, out
toward the Atlantic's darker waters
the pelicans keep drifting . . .

What is it we keep thinking of?
Of the brilliance of some perfect noon
arrived now from its opaque distance?
Or of the doctor, half our age,
who will stare down into the shallows
of our eyes, then turn to mark
his chart, as the soul begins to slip now
through the fissure of the mouth?

It is what we often think about,
though we mask it any way we can,
to think instead of sunlight in Miami,
as in a painting by the poet Donald
Justice, which shows the keylime
cobalt brilliance of the surging
gulf, and in the background
three dots drifting slowly out to sea . . .

THE GREAT ASSEMBLY

Numberless crowded streets, high growths of iron, slender,
strong, light, splendidly uprising toward clear skies . . .
Immigrants arriving, fifteen or twenty thousand in a week . . .
WALT WHITMAN, "Mannahatta"

In immense golden spokes the broken light
filters in upon the children gathered
in the great assembly hall of the yellow
brick gradeschool on Fifty-first and First.
It is 1946 and the long war is over.

He stands there at attention as he has
been told to by his teacher, and stares up
at the broad stripes & bright stars,
the bunched notes of the anthem breaking
all around him. Out in the harbor the green

colossus is still holding up her arm, calling
to the poor & tempest-tossed. To this teeming
city once they came, his parents' parents,
queuing like the others through Ellis Island:
wops, gaptoothed Swedes, displaced Russian Poles.

Everywhere gray pigeons brood on sills
and tarpitched roofs, peck by peck eating
the city's dirt. This afternoon there will be
the German-Irish gang to contend with
as they fan out below the El like jackals.

He knows they mean to hurt him any way
they can if only they can catch him.
Last week they unfurled the billowing bloodred
banner with its twisted black cross opposite
the brownstone synagogue, then tore across

the tarred roofs with a fat cop wheezing after.
Yesterday it was an outraged three-piece suit
who wedged his foot up into the groin of a drunk
who had exposed himself, while the drunk's wife
begged the man to stop. On and on it goes. And still

the light flows on in a great unflowing. Each day
brings something new for him to learn, part
of the grand design it seems is meant for him.
As here, in the Great Assembly, with the music
of the morning anthem breaking all around him.

DUET

Noon: the Jones Beach causeway
shimmering in the August haze,
the hoods of overheated Fords
& Packards, Depression black, and by
the thousands, stalled in traffic.
My brother, sister & myself in back,
my mother with the baby on her lap
up front, my father inching forward
as if still testing Shermans
for the Army. She tried to salvage
things by turning up the radio
to sing, my mother, for she sang
beautifully, and she was beautiful
and young. She kept coaxing him
to sing along with her, her bell-bright
voice & his in harmony. A duet.
Bass & alto. The male & female of it.
But there he was, my father, leaning
on his horn as someone tried
to inch around him. Then that someone
shouting through my father's window,
my mother pleading, my father out
the door, then back & vindicated. . . .

Forty years, forty years, and still
I see her, her lips pale and shaken
in the rearview mirror as we sat there
stunned & silent. By then the music
on the radio was gone. Gone too
whatever song she had been singing,
ground down again first to a sound
like bearings scraping, then tears,
then after that to nothing.

SAYING GOODBYE

At a signal from the undertaker's
young assistant, we lift the stubborn
metal casket, and I—as oldest son
and most unwilling emissary—lead
my sons & brothers to the plush cover
of the new-dug grave.

                So this is how
it ends. With a backhoe idling
behind a row of maples, its driver
impatient to be home for dinner. And this:
a green tent sighing high above a pit,
words about the Resurrection choking
the claustrophobic air.

                   And now
I catch my father standing off there
to the side, his second wife beside him,
eyes gazing at the crumpled distance.
And now, ever so gently, my right hand
strokes the bronze side of her casket,
about where her pillowed head would be,
and suddenly I am whispering to her. "There,
there, Momma," I am saying, "it's all right
now. Everything is going to be just fine."

HORSES

for WYATT PRUNTY

Late afternoon & late summer light, a scene
shaped by forty years of prismatic memory,
transforming barn & straw & an old man
with his girls—three mares & a tired sullen pony—
into something neither boy had ever seen before,

as they watched the old man in the stall below
counting out his money: two rolls of faded singles,
two leather sacks fat with dimes & nickles. . . .
Here in his room, alone now, after all these years,
he must listen to it all again: the clink of coins,

the rustling bills, the swish of the mare's tail
in the dry heat of September as it flicked against
the blue blur of the flies' incessant buzzing.
For three days the old man's leathery face, grim,
unsmiling, beneath his sweat-stained rim, as he led

his girls round & round the tamped grass circle,
the children giddy, the children braving it
as they rode the horses' backs for dimes & nickels. . . .
He remembers the still-unpolluted clam beds
of the island's plum majestic beaches, carriage houses

cut off now from their bulldozed mansions, the ghostly
aria of the whippoorwill echoing through the marshes.
But most of all an old man kneeling beside the open
whiskey bottle, surrounded by his girls, as he hid
his money in a hollow in the straw, then stumbled out

to catch the setting sun, while the boys, emboldened
by their knowledge, climbed down to tear through
the blazing straw, each after his mess of coins
& singles, then disappeared into the shadows,
the sad brown eyes of the horses straining after.

GHOST

After so much time you think
you'd have it netted
in the mesh of language. But again
it reconfigures, slick as Proteus.

You're in the kitchen talking
with your ex-Navy brother, his two kids
snaking over his tattooed arms, as he goes on
& on about being out of work again.

For an hour now you've listened,
his face growing dimmer in the lamplight
as you keep glancing at your watch
until it's there again: the ghost rising

as it did that first time when you,
the oldest, left home to marry.
You're in the boat again, alone, and staring
at the six of them, your sisters

& your brothers, their faces bobbing
in the water, as their fingers grapple
for the gunwales. The ship is going down,
your mother with it. One oar's locked

and feathered, and one oar's lost,
there's a slop of gurry pooling
in the bottom, and your tiny boat
keeps drifting further from them.

Between each bitter wave you can count
their upturned faces—white roses
scattered on a mash of sea, eyes fixed
to see what you will do. And you?

You their old protector, you their guardian
and go-between? *Each man for himself,*
you remember thinking, their faces
growing dimmer with each oarstroke.

II

THE MUSIC OF DESIRE

Having done his best and lost her anyway
to someone with a car & cash, try
as he will he cannot shut out the unbearable
high haunting trumpet tones spilling
from the wooden radio half hidden
by the broccoli and fan. All this long autumn
afternoon he has kept busy dusting shelves,
having three times swept the aisles
of Danny Rossi's family grocery store,
as he watches the only customers he's had
for hours: two twelve year-olds trying
to swipe an *Argosy* from the five-tiered
comic rack where someone with her grayblue eyes
smiles sadly from the cover.

       He drums his fingers
on the candy counterpane, then the register,
and waits. And still the trumpet intervenes,
wailing of a loss as recent as his own
and yet as old (as even he can see)
as those youthful couples etched
on Attic cenotaphs on the ghostwhite
screen in Art 11: a loss as ancient
as the human heart itself.

       But for now
it will do no good to try and distance
such insatiable and overwhelming hungers.
The girl he loved is gone, an old song
surely, repeated every moment of every
single day, somewhere in the world,
the way the consecration is everywhere
repeated, as Fr. Hagen used to love to say.
Which is to say that somewhere, always,
someone tastes the awful bite of unlove
and of loss.

As now, with the last notes
of a solitary horn fading in the impassioned
regal sun which has had a billion years
to learn to fall from grace without a grumble,
unlike the scene from some provincial
tragedy it has been witness to here
in Danny Rossi's family grocery store.

MANHATTAN

for ROBERT CREELEY

Thirty years, and the six-inch scar still there
like a white & leprous flower. Five beers
& five Manhattans at this college bar
in Hempstead & then south with Peers
& Wilbur to the White Castle as I chatter
on about my Ethics test & how Aquinas avers
means can be said to justify the ends (or
is it ends means?) when they're there,
this one in stud leather who insists on star-
ing at my *Manhattan College* jacket. And before
I know it, we're out behind the building, under
the springtime stars, both staggering, stud leather
leering & coming at me, until in sheer terror
I tear into him, fists knotted in his greasy hair,
smashing his head against the blacktop border.
And in two minutes it's over, & through a blur
of cheers I'm downing five Manhattans more,
then swimming upstreet through some phosphor glare
to steal a men's sign for some faceless stranger,
ten feet of coiled barbed wire having so far
stopped him.   But nothing can stop Manhattan, no sir,
and halfway up the pole razor teeth shear
my leg to lace & then I'm down. And when I pare
back an eyelid the morning after, pain is everywhere,
and there's this ugly fishmouth wound down there,
and I'm tearing past my mother, & at 9:05 I glare
at Ethics Question 1, then down at my bloody cor-
duroys & across at Self-loathing & old friend Fear,
both already bored, & yawning at whatever answer
I come up with for Questions 2 & 3 & 4.

BROTHERHOOD

Week one we went from sixteen
down to four & signed a kamikaze
pact between us not to quit.
I shaved my head so close that

Brother Paul, lecturing contrabasso
on the dizzy driftings of Ulysses,
lifted his heavy brows & ceased
mid-dactyl to inquire of my lice.

Worse still the girls shunning
the four of us at parties, except
to stare as we served them drinks
or wrote them stupid verses on consignment.

Dogs too avoided us. On campus
we had to don painter's caps
so preternaturally white even
the frat sadist with his whiskey-tumbler-

bulls-eye glasses could spot us
slouching across the tree-lined quad.
Each noon in one of the quonset huts
on campus, a silverback gorilla

wacked an oak paddle up & down
the pink insides of our thighs.
The brothers tired, edgy, drunk.
Somehow we kept failing them.

To teach us, they used hurling sticks
across our cringing backsides: ash-hard,
curved, unsplittable. Pain so intense
Swinburne would have loved it.

Then, in mid-November, two hours
north in a dilapidated DeSoto:
a final weekend in the Catskills,
a huddled mass of eight arms

and as many legs gone beyond even
terror, exhausted, crawling through
a makeshift Via Dolorosa made up
of hay, beer, mud & horseshit.

And all for what? To say the Test
was passed? To listen mooneyed
to initiation rites while a candle
on a cardboard altar sputtered?

So that, black-assed, we might limp
together down to the Greenleaf Bar
to swap stories of some mythic
predecessor's twelve-inch dong?

Here's to the two-year reign
of brotherhood forever, when we drank
until our shirts turned stiff with vomit.
When we stared in dismal stupefaction

as a brother fumbled with his date,
pleading for a blowjob, before he toppled
through a Harlem dancehall window.
Here's too to all those brothers

(including one sadist & a gorilla)
I ferried home each Friday night for nothing,
my brother's maladaptive brakeless Chevy
weaving back & forth across Manhattan

& the Bronx & Queens & Brooklyn & yes
even farflung Staten Island, as we drifted
in the going round of wheels, and croaked
our hearts out to the empty hunter moon.

HARRY

And as we hear you do reform yourselves,
We will, according to your strengths and qualities,
Give you advancement.

HENRY *IV*, Part 2

The paisley kerchief blooming
from his breast pocket, the greengray
Windsorknotted tie, the chain looped
across the waist, the hornrimmed glasses.
Harry's impeccable lectures on myne own
Sir Philip Sidney, the Perfect Courtier,
offering his cup of water to the broken
private when he himself lay dying
beneath the arching lowlands tree. Harry,
dead these twenty years, striding high then
across the lightlaced inner quad,
a French text in his tanned & perfumed hand.
Harry, with the Army Corps of Engineers
at Remagen that spring of '45.
Were those pearls he strew
before Monahan, McCormick, Walsh, & me
as he lectured on until the very angels
must have wept? Soldier, scholar, statesman,
poet, prince. The very thing itself.

Before the tarnished hallway
mirror, I aped his walk, his talk,
the half-tilt of that aristocratic shoulder.
At last, seeing that even the junk trees
along the fence were breaking into blossom,
I screwed the courage up to ask
for help in going on to grad school.
"Though I have come late to English, Harry,"
the words rehearsed for weeks, *"help me.*
I will not let you down."

And then to watch him turn away
that lovely sculpted head of his
& hear him say it, *no, how he was sorry,*
but he couldn't, no. And then,
but for the intervening thirty years
of holding up one's end of the aborted
bargain, that was all. Except to smile
one's embarrassed, crooked smile
& turn away oneself, as on my Harry rushed,
intent on getting where he had to go.

WORLD OF OUR FATHERS

for IRVING HOWE

Your serpentine smile, Lowell dubbed it back
in '68, the year you wrote *New York Intellectual*,
that last salute to a grand ideal already seaworn
as the shell of the old moon wasting westward.

How well I recall that smile, Irving, those years
I listened to your clipped lectures on the tragic
pathos that seemed to follow you even to the 14th
floor of Hunter College with its unforgiving off-white

bus-station decor, your fine ear distressed by the honking
from the streets below which threatened to invade this,
your Axel's Castle, your last redoubt. "When they come
to write my life," you said, "tell them it was this

which finally killed me." How, I wondered, could one
ever penetrate your polished, iced-over urban sheen?
And how had a Jewish kid from the Depression Bronx
ever settled on that Cambridge Thirties accent more

outrageously pronounced even than your friend Berryman's?
A dazzler, Irving, was what you were, though you had
a penchant for dismissal easily the match of Nemerov's
("This paper is struggling to become two essays.

Divide it here. Then throw away both halves").
Your eye, fixed on some unsuspecting student
in the cafeteria, withering to ash whatever argument
he might have mustered: "Why is *Jane Eyre* a classic?

Because it is." Each of my boiling neo-Emersonian
papers came back from you without a comment, the last
page each time branded with the same blue-circled B.
Irving, I used to dream of *being* you: knitbrowed,

bespectacled, a blue pencil dangling magisterially
in my right hand as I too read my galleys, at long
last tenured, like you someday pulling in my Persian
twenty grand a year. At my comps you might easily

have broken me with any of your far-ranging,
fine-honed probing questions, your inquisitorial eye
behind those steel bifocals fixed on my more furtive
gaze, before inexplicably allowing me to pass out

into the wide world beyond to teach composition
to the sons & daughters of stenographers & cops.
And now you too are gone and I am left behind,
I, the least of your disciples, and, like Nicodemus,

a secret one at that. Far too centrist, you would have
said, and certainly one who never found the courage
to pick up telephone or pen to thank you for those
napalm-spattered maxims whose scars still itch.

For years after I lost sight of you. Nixon
and the hundred years' war were history by the time
we met again, of all unlikely places in the Russian
Tea Room to clink a glass to our dear friend, Allen.

By then, old warrior, the wheel had come full circle.
Age had mellowed even you into a grinning rabbi
flush with jokes & stories, your great work honoring
the lost world of your fathers by now behind you.

In the rafters one could just make out those thin ghosts
bantering back & forth in Yiddish, while you played
your willing audience of one like some old vaudeville
comic who comes at last to play the part he loves.

THE STATUE

for ALLEN MANDELBAUM

A July evening, *venti anni fa,* the four of us:
Laura, Eileen, myself, moon-eyed New World pilgrims
on a Monday, in our Audi, with our delicious guide,
our Allen, up the steep mountain pass which leads

into Sulmona. Across from the Hotel Traffico
where we stayed that night, facing the Piazza
Venti Settembre, the only foreigners as far
as we could tell, loomed Ovid's bronzeblack statue.

Church bells rang their going on the evening air:
a semibasso eight followed by a flatter three.
The soft laughter of the strollers, arms about each
other, as it drifted on the hilltop currents.

All changed to air, thin air, except what Allen
taught me on that journey, not knowing he was teaching:
the exquisite patience of the man, this Englisher
of Homer, Virgil, Dante, & the moderns, straining hour

after hour for three baffled monoglots, so that
one might eat the bistecca of one's desire
rather than the tripe & ink squid one's language
had concocted. A kerchief dipped into the icy mountain

runnel & placed on Eileen's forehead, where we
had stopped beside the ruined farmhouse like the one
Horace speaks of in his letters, while I paced up
& down beside the car, clueless to her pain,

impatient for her color to return. The look
he flashed me then through those thick-rimmed glasses
which had seen so much, light blazing into darkness,
the way angels, he once told me, address each other.

As on the morning of our departure from Sulmona,
when I looked up from my coffee to catch him
standing there, his eyes already on his statue,
having crossed eighty generations to have it out

with that grand old polytheist, seachanging Ovid,
Sad-Seigneur-of-Scrutinists, his glittering,
redrimmed eyes aglint once more, while Ovid's
shifting bronzeblack surface glinted back.

QUID PRO QUO

Just after my wife's miscarriage (her second
in four months), I was sitting in an empty
classroom exchanging notes with my friend,
a budding Joyce scholar with steelrimmed
glasses, when, lapsed Irish Catholic that he was,
he surprised me by asking what I thought now
of God's ways toward man. It was spring,

such spring as came to the flintbacked Chenango
Valley thirty years ago, the full force of Siberia
behind each blast of wind. Once more my poor wife
was in the local four-room hospital, recovering.
The sun was going down, the room's pinewood panels
all but swallowing the gelid light, when, suddenly,
I surprised not only myself but my colleague

by raising my middle finger up to heaven, *quid
pro quo,* the hardly grand defiant gesture a variant
on Vanni Fucci's figs, shocking not only my friend
but in truth the gesture's perpetrator too. I was 24,
and, in spite of having pored over the *Confessions*
& that Catholic Tractate called the *Summa,* was sure
I'd seen enough of God's erstwhile ways toward man.

That summer, under a pulsing midnight sky
shimmering with Van Gogh stars, in a creaking,
cedarscented cabin off Lake George, having lied
to the gentrified owner of the boys' camp
that indeed I knew wilderness & lakes and could,
if need be, lead a whole fleet of canoes down
the turbulent whitewater passages of the Fulton Chain

(I who had last been in a rowboat with my parents
at the age of six), my wife and I made love, trying
not to disturb whosever headboard & waterglass
lie just beyond the paperthin partition at our feet.
In the great black Adirondack stillness, as we lay
there on our sagging mattress, my wife & I gazed out
through the broken roof into a sky that seemed

somehow to look back down on us, and in that place,
that holy place, she must have conceived again,
for nine months later in a New York hospital she
brought forth a son, a little buddha-bellied
rumplestiltskin runt of a man who burned
to face the sun, the fact of his being there
both terrifying & lifting me at once, this son,

this gift, whom I still look upon with joy & awe. Worst,
best, just last year, this same son, grown
to manhood now, knelt before a marble altar to vow
everything he had to the same God I had had my own
erstwhile dealings with. How does one bargain
with a God like this, who, *quid pro quo,* ups
the ante each time He answers one sign with another?

THEN

Glint of mahogany, glint of those pulsing
neon lights, the far shadows in the barroom
buzzing, as he rehearsed the byzantine
stratagems by which he might address her,
afraid she too would fade like all the others. . . .

Scalloped hair, blue eyes, blossoming white blouse,
this brightness, this Proserpine glimpsed
for the first time thirty years ago. The night sky
clear for once above the streets of Mineola, with
here and there a star. His Beta Sigma brothers, to whom
he had just sworn eternal solidarity, off
in the next room already growing dimmer. . . .

She sits across the room from him, bifocals
intent upon her book, head bent as if weighted down,
this woman he has shared a life with. . . . Can he call her
back as she was then? Can he rewrite their tangled
history as he would have it, now the plot
draws nearer to its close? The mind, the aging mind,
which must one day see itself extinguished. . . .

Expecting nothing, he found her there, there
in a pub, on the corner of Williston & Jericho,
in quotidian Mineola, in the midst of Gaudelli,
Ritchie, Walsh, and all the other hearts,
on a Friday night in mid-December, at the dull end
of the Eisenhower years, his third semester over. . . .

How can such gifts be, he wonders, even
as he looks up from his book to catch sight
of the blossoms just outside his window:
great masses of late June blossoms, white
on white on white, flaring from the shagged catalpa
that seems dead half of every year, until against
the odds the very air around is turned to whiteness.

III

THE GODS WHO COME AMONG US
IN THE GUISE OF STRANGERS

for CHARLIE MILLER

Late nights, with summer moths clinging
to the screens & the shadows of the Old Great
flickering across the tv screen, suddenly,
there would be Charlie's inquisitorial head
peering in the window, the shock of white hair,
followed by the heart-stopping shock
of greeting. Just passing through, he'd say,
and—seeing as the light was on—
thought we might have ourselves a talk.

Did I ever have time enough for Charlie?
Usually not. The story of my life,
of the one, as Chaucer says of someone,
who seems always busier than he is.
Then, abruptly, & discourteously,
death put a stop to Charlie's visits.
Summer moths collect still at the windows.
Then leaves & winter ice. Then summer moths
again. Each year, old ghost, I seem
to miss you more and more, your youth spent
with Auden & the Big Ones, words—
theirs, yours—helping you survive
a brutal youth. Too late I see now
how you honored me like those hidden
gods of old who walk among us like
the dispossessed, and who, if you are
among the lucky ones, tap at your window
when you least expect to ask you for a cup
of water and a little of your time.

THE REPUBLIC

for DAVID IGNATOW

Midnight. For the past three hours
I've raked over Plato's *Republic*
with my students, all of them John
Jay cops, and now some of us
have come to Rooney's to unwind.
Boilermakers. Double shots and triples.
Fitzgerald's still in his undercover
clothes and giveaway white socks, and two
lieutenants—Seluzzi in the sharkskin suit
& D'Ambruzzo in the leather—have just
invited me to catch their fancy (and illegal)
digs somewhere up in Harlem, when
this cop begins to tell his story:

how he and his partner trailed
this pusher for six weeks before
they trapped him in a burnt-out
tenement somewhere down in SoHo,
one coming at him up the stairwell,
the other up the fire escape
and through a busted window. But by
the time they've grabbed him
he's standing over an open window
and he's clean. The partner races down
into the courtyard and begins going
through the garbage until he finds
what it is he's after: a white bag
hanging from a junk mimosa like
the Christmas gift it is, and which now
he plants back on the suspect.
Cross-examined by a lawyer who does his best
to rattle them, he and his partner
stick by their story, and the charges stick.

Fitzgerald shrugs. Business as usual.
But the cop goes on. Better to let
the guy go free than under oath
to have to lie like that.
And suddenly you can hear the heavy
suck of air before Seluzzi, who
half an hour before was boasting
about being on the take, staggers
to his feet, outraged at what he's heard,
and insists on taking the bastard
downtown so they can book him.

Which naturally brings to an end
the discussion we've been having,
and soon each of us is heading
for an exit, embarrassed by the awkward
light the cop has thrown on things.
Which makes it clearer now to me why
the State would offer someone like Socrates
a shot of hemlock. And even clearer
why Socrates would want to drink it.

THE CISTERN

In the limestone cistern
beneath St. Peter Gallicantu
in Jerusalem, my back against
the wall, try as I might,
I could not keep from weeping.
I am a man gone down into the pit,
we listened to Fr. Doyle reading,
a man shorn of his strength,
one more among the dead,
among those You have forgotten.

And did he call upon the psalms
to warm him in his need?
The night before he died
they dragged him here to try him.
What answers he could give
lay shattered on the pavement.
Later his quizzers grew tired
and impatient. Let others try him
in the morning. Enough for now
to knot a rope across his chest
and drop him into darkness.

Hanging by his wrists, *Eli,*
he would cry out, *Eli,* and again
they would misread him, thinking
he was calling on Elijah.
As each of us will be: alone,
friends scattered to the winds.
Except for one out in the courtyard
growing cold, poised now to deny him.
Darkness, the psalmist ended.
The one companion left me.

LIEUTENANT OWEN

This then was where it waited: in mist,
in cold November rain, trying to get
his men past yet another flooded trench.
Back & forth he stumbled, a small man,
old at twenty-five. His hand reached

to touch their shoulders as they ran past
toward the chill machinegun-riddled waters,
the gray shapes out there waiting. "*Well done,*"
he cheered them on, "*well done, my boys,*"
as a teacher might, or as a father.

The letters home all written, the poems,
the last *i* dotted. What there was to say
he'd said. At the trench's edge he could
just make out the duckboards, already
splintered by the tic tic from the other bank.

And now Kirk down with a bullet to the head,
and now the Colonel, & Sapper York
& Topping, the memory too of Private
Jones's blood like a grotesque smear
of lipstick down his shoulder. It was then,

as he knelt to right one of the boards,
wet hands parrying with the awful cold,
that his lips parted in a daze of expectation,
and the only thing still left for him to find
he found waiting for him on that distant shore.

THE BOMBINGS

for JOHN

It's not the kids, he chokes into the phone.
They're not the problem. Chicanos,
most of them. Tough & raw & proud,
with a peppering of blacks & whites
& Papagos, & all in trouble with the law.

Tucson's fine, the work's fine, even
the desert has begun to bloom. No,
it's the same nightmare night after
night, where he must watch a giant ram
a midget's head against a wall.

Again the giant rams it, again, again,
waiting for the midget to shout uncle,
even as the midget scrambles for the English
word for uncle. What's worse, he says,
is that the kids he works with look exactly

like this midget. Two thousand miles away,
and he wants to know what he should do.
What was I thinking when I urged him
out into the world, the same world I fled from
all those years ago? I, whose hometown saws

could comfort no one, least of all a son
out in the desert, who dreams nightly now
of the giant's endless pounding, until he feels
the sagging beams above him snap, and a light,
phosphor white & unforgiving, burns away the dark.

January–February 1991

THE MILLENARIANS

The voiceover on the grainy film
explaining how the president was shot,
his wife, too, shot in the cobblestoned
courtyard on Christmas Day by members
of the people's army. Children haunt
the crumbling concrete factories, and every
fourth citizen has become a paid informer.
The nightly blackouts go to light
the presidential palace, a fungal growth
already larger than Versailles.

Forty years ago the schoolbooks showed
a red tide spreading over half the world,
atop which stalked a Russian bear, medieval,
looming, something out of Nostradamus.
The wheel of history ground down
to a standstill, the living language with it.

On the oaktop kitchen table in this gelid
light: two amplebottomed glass containers,
in which float the white filaments
of exposed nerve ends. Above these:
forced clusters of royal purple hyacinth
twisting slowly toward each other.

Out in the mothering winter dawn
the jays are already at it, screaming
from the gnarled branches at finch
and moody wooddove to steer clear
until they've had their fill.
But the doves are hungry too and will not
budge. The more the bandits scream
the more the others hunker down, half
deaf & half iced over, but stubborn,
& rooted to their crusts of precious earth.

A SEPARATE PEACE

He stared out from the tangled
bine stems & the winter trees into
the fog to find the shadows there
of boys with shotguns. He was here
to search for rebels, "bandits"
who had forced the people into fighting.
Instead, all he saw were people.

It seemed like Stalingrad all over,
except that it was he who was the enemy.
To fight would mean more losses
for his men, like the two already cold
or the two holding their broken heads
& moaning. And these were soldiers
under him, paratroopers, their motto,
"We can die, but we won't give up."

But he was tired now, tired of all
this desperate Rambo posturing.
Too many disaffected frontline officers
back from the Afghan deserts deepwired
with despair. Too many ambushes, too many
homemade booby traps, too many legs
turned instantly to mist. In the deserted
cobbled streets, packdogs sniffed out
his comrades' shrouded bodies. True,
they could take hostages, push north
to link up with the army.

And all for what? Already mothers
were flocking in from Moscow
to take their soldiers home, even
if they had to pull them by the ears.
If he got back from this one,
it meant Siberia . . . or worse.
But a separate peace would mean
a chance of going home again,
he and the men there with him,
back to the smell of bread & meat,
back to people very much like these,
except for the shattered faces.

PILGRIM

"As the watchman waits for the dawn . . . "

I think of Jimmy Pellegrino as always
at attention, watching over both his
daughters with that hawklike vigilance
of his, and of Edith, his wife of fifty
years, ever eager to please her family,
chattering as she stirred her magic sauces.
A tenement in Brooklyn, a house and lawn
in Hempstead. Jimmy selling plastic toys,
dapper Jim selling suits and shoes.
I think of him returning from the war,
his feet still somehow in his shoes,
who had nearly lost them in the fighting
in the Ardennes. "My darling Edith," he wrote
from an English hospital in the spring
of '45, both feet still black and swollen,
"I am getting better, and think only
of coming home to you and our little girl."
Last year, his lungs gone, tubes running
from his nose, he watched helplessly
as Edith wandered through the house,
her mind drifting more and more each day.
More than once he must have thought
of going out the way his buddies had, alone
and wounded in their shallow trenches,
and slowly freezing, while German snipers
watched their every movement through their scopes.
Now it was he who watched, as he lay there
listening to her breathing in the bed
beside him. His lovely Edith, who no longer
seemed to know him. What was left him now
but to lace his boots up one last time
and reconnoiter in those woods beyond
the river, where he would wait to take
his Edith to the cabin in the clearing
he was being sent ahead to find.

ONE DARK NIGHT

"Noche Oscura": Juan de la Cruz

One dark night,
burning with love's deep hungers,
    —oh happy happy chance!—
    the whole house asleep at last,
I slipped away unnoticed.

In darkness, in safety,
disguised, down a secret ladder
    —oh happy happy chance!—
    hidden by darkness,
the whole house asleep at last.

On that happy happy night,
in secret, when no one saw me
    and I saw nothing,
    with no other light for guide
than the one that blazed away inside me. . . .

And yet it guided me
more surely than the sun at noon
    to where He waited for me
    —he whom I knew so well—
to where no one could disturb us.

Oh guiding night.
Night sweeter than the dawn.
    Oh night that mingled
    lover and beloved,
when she was changed forever by her lover. . . .

On my blossoming breast,
which I had saved for him alone,
	he lay there sleeping
	all the while I caressed him
as scented cedars, swaying, fanned the air.

	Down from the tower walls breezes floated
all the while I lay there playing with his hair.
	Oh so tenderly then his hand
	bent back my neck,
numbing all my senses.

	I lay there then forgetting who I was,
my face flush against my lover's,
	until everything stopped turning,
	and self faded from itself, faded too my cares,
until among the lilies even they were soon forgotten.

IV

MOUNTAIN VIEW WITH FIGURES

As if Cézanne had rendered it: a palimpsest
of planes, a dreamscape realized, an imbrication,
the easel facing the brilliant south exposure.

In the middle foreground a patch of vale, shadowed
by a swirl of crosshatched pines. He counts again
the colors: a tan, a green, a gray, a tan, a tan.

Beyond the graygreen strokes he feels the Absolute
malignly beckon in the bald & treeless peaks.
He stares now as he contemplates his labors,

the hesitations hissing up ahead. It is
what has kept him sleepless night after night:
fear at the edge of the abyss, empty speculations

deep enough for even an Empedocles. He knows
the most he has to paint with is a round
of absinthe sounds & acrobatic stanzas. Those

and a syntax even the boys at the Sorbonne
could nod assent to. He wants the words to paint
his naked canvas, words to ring in the Absolute

at last. He wants to feel the mountain ring.
Fool that he is, he needs to feel that, if he
climbed it now, he would find himself transfigured.

LANDSCAPE WITH DOG

Often up the back steps he came
bearing gifts: frozen squirrels,
sodden links of sausage, garter
snakes, the odd sneaker. The gnarled
marks are still there as witness that,
confined, he took his tensions out
on doors & tables. And life went on,
& mornings, peace & war, good times
& depressions. Pale sticks turned
to trees, boys to larger boys, then men.
Icestorms, wakes, elections came & went.
And always he was there, like air,
a good wife. But then there's this

to think about & think about again:
the last time I saw Sparky he was dying.
His legs trembled & he kept moping
after me. I remember trying to get
the stubborn mower started, June blazing
& grease & six-inch grass & sweat,
& no time then to stop to pet a dog.
And having no time left himself,
Sparky simply lifted off those
cog-wheel scrawny legs of his,
& turned, one of the best things
life ever handed me, and lay down
somewhere in the woods to die.

NEW ENGLAND WINTER

To hell with John Greenleaf Whittier
and his chirpy snowfall odes. Snow.
We've had our share: 18 storms thus far,
ice layered like so much sandstone shale.
A regular archaeologist's dig.
All the television graphics show
this at least: a winter made in hell.
Each day now proud old records fall,

to be replaced by miserable new ones.
What fun it is to sit here counting
off minus 30 mornings, these glittering
kitchen pipes festooned with ice.
On the upside, take the Angelinos after
last's month's quake, fear mounting
with the mounting Richter Scale,
the decibels revised upward. Twice.

"Maybe, but I'll still take the quake's
twenty seconds to your hundred-day
glacial siege. *Anytime.*" Thus my
California sister, who *can* be tough.
What hoürs, days, I have spent.
reading the West Coast fault lines from L.A.
on up, all the way to the Aleutian chain.
"At least we're built on firmer stuff,"

I feel myself edging to a crushing
rejoinder, this once vindicated. But by then
she's off the phone, no doubt
outdoors already, tanning on that delicious
cedar-toasted deck of hers which gazes
so serenely out over the Pacific Ocean.
While here am I, iced-over & snowed under,
blinking out this frozen glass. At this.

WORDS

for Barry Moser

Midwinter. A coalmining town
somewhere in Pennsylvania. A man
walks pensively an icy street
in darkness. Everything is dark,
except for the sheet of windblown
foolscap, which seems to move
the same way he is moving,
until at last he feels compelled
to stoop and pick it up.

How surprised he is to find
a poem there on the crumpled sheet,
words scribbled down in pencil,
slantwise, half of them misspelt,
but fierce words still, huddled
there before him against the cold
like so much coalblue mummy corn,
the germ inside waiting for this eye,
this ear, to grow inside the man.

The man can see the words have shaped
the awkward air of the occasion, and are
the soundings of some wounded soul,
a soul charred perhaps by too much drink,
though it might be any wound—fear,
loneliness, remorse—needing to be
embraced and taken in, which is what
the man, who warms his hands before
the broken words, now begins to do.

MOONRISE AS ABSTRACTION

Last night, driving west along the parkway
toward the hospital, I watched the old moon
struggling to lift itself above the tangled treeline.

The oncoming lights blurred large & ominous,
whirred past, then curved away. Bare branches
stretched their fingers upward, black etched

against the silver black. The pockmarked craters
of the old moon's eyes stared past me until
I understood at last my friend was dying.

There was a grinding in the going round of wheels
as the busy lights rushed up again to meet me.
Except for the preternatural brilliance of his eyes,

he would be a shadow only, the waning of a light
which for a time had eclipsed the other lights around,
a light egyptian, regal, unlike the common

string of traffic lights approaching, though
for a while yet he would be closer than the cold
and distant stars. In the darkened room

on the sixth floor of the hospital, his eyes
would still be fixed upon the game, as if
the outcome really mattered anymore, when

what mattered was that he was going to a place
I could not follow, at least not yet, though
I'd prayed to keep him from that final journey west.

And then it came: something like an answer, as the
wheels beneath my feet rounded yet another bend,
and I looked up to see the moon shake free of the mesh

of trees like the solitary king he is, and felt
myself unclench into a gesture of goodbye, as if
now at last my friend might ease me on my way.

THE GREAT WHEEL

In the Tuileries we came upon the Great Wheel
rising gargantuan above the trees. Evening
was coming on. An after-dinner stroll, descending
by easy stages toward the river, a bridge of leaves
above us, broken here and there by street lights
coming on. Our time here nearly over, our return

home a shadow hovering. Paris, city of returns,
you said, for the pleasure of it, like the Great Wheel
looming there above us, all steel & light
& music, daredevil daunting, against the evening
sky with the tower in the distance winking. The leaves
still held firmly, the unthinkable descending

of what lay ahead undreamt of still, death descending
inevitably as the Great Wheel in its return,
(a descent first through summer's golden leaves
and then bare ruined branches), the Great Wheel
turning & returning. As then, with the all but evening
over us, our wives laughing by the entrance lights,

we rose above the mansard roofs, the trees, the lights,
lifting in a vertiginous ascent before descending,
as we chattered on against the coming on of evening,
our seat creaking in the rising wind, anxious to return
now to earth's solidities. Instead, the Great Wheel
merely sighed and lifted, stopping at the top, leaving

each of us alone now with our thoughts. The leaves
below, green, graygreen, gray, the dollhouse roofs, lights
like diamonds winking, aloof & distant, the Great Wheel
playing us, two middle-aged men, each descending
toward the Wheel's one appointed end, the Great Return
to earth, as the books all have it, come our evening.

For all our feigned bravado, we could feel the evening
over us, even as we stared down upon the blur of leaves,
our wives, our distant children, on all we would return
to, the way shipwrecked sailors search for lights
along a distant shore, as we began the last descent,
leaving the tents and Garden with its Great Wheel

to return, my dear dead friend, to the winking lights
along the boulevard, leaves lifting & descending,
as now the evening air took mastery, it & the Great Wheel.

VOYAGER

Beyond the moon, beyond planet blue
and planet red, each day further
from the sun she floats out toward

the empty dark of X. Having done
what she was sent out years before
to do, she gave up sending even

the faintest signals back to earth,
to bend instead her shattered wings
across her breast for warmth. It is

late, he knows, and knows it will only
go on getting later. He shifts alone
in the late November light before

her grave, as so often he has done
these past five years, to try
and finish what he knows to be

unfinished business and must remain
that way: this one-way dialogue
between the self, and—in her absence—

the mother in himself. Epilogue, perhaps,
to what one man might do to heal
the shaken ghost which must at last admit

just how many years ago she logged off
on her journey. So that now, as darkness
drops about him like some discarded coat,

old but useful, such as his mother used
to wear, he takes it to him, much as
she did, to ward against the cold.

AND THIS THY HARBOR

He said, "This water flows east down . . . to the sea; and
flowing into the sea it makes its waters wholesome.
Wherever the river flows, all living creatures teeming
in it will live. . . . Along the river, on either bank,
will grow every kind of fruit tree with leaves that
never wither and fruit that never fails . . . because this
water comes from the sanctuary. And their fruit will be
good to eat and the leaves medicinal.

Once, twenty years before, he'd sung
into the cold wind playing the meshed
steel cables of the bridge, and listened
as the East River began its merging
with the Atlantic's vast & patient heart.

Something he must have seen there
in the river, something to make him lift
his voice in song. Or so the story goes.
Did he still wear puttees? His soft wool
army cap, his khaki coat, as in the photo,

with the campaign ribbon from his year
in France? Harry. Harry Green, my mother's
father. Thirty-three, and already marked
with the mustard wound that would soon stop
his singing altogether. . . .

At seven, lungs filling with the raw
fresh air the city offers all her children
freely, I found myself straying from
the park entrance off 51st down to that
same dark river, where I perched above

the drenched rocks in the cataleptic light
of 1947. By then my mother's father
had been dead for fifteen years. A man
in a filthy coat stood on those rocks
above the moiling waters, pointing a derringer

at nothing in particular. Gulls still circled
for whatever they could glean from the city's
sleepless leavings. Where the man's mouth had been
a rictus now was forming as he took aim
and fired, the gulls wheeling in a flash of fury

as the sky in that sudden instant shattered.
I might have turned then like any other child
to scramble for the shoulder of the FDR,
the park, the gate, the brindled sycamores.
Instead, according to the story, it was then

I chose to take my stand, exactly as the angel
in the Gospel of St. Dismas is said
to have, our two mouths opening in unison
onto caves of holy song, both of us unwilling
any longer to bear mute witness to the darkness

which seeks to shatter everything, the light
of our chime-capped notes restoring each
thing to its primal brilliance: the broken
figures in a thousand grainy boxcars,
the ashen dead among the city's alleys,

the stunned trenches where no birds sing,
as in that instant our song made whole again
the river, & the benzined brilliance
of the gulls, the lost song Harry sang once
by these waters rising from the waters with him.

ANTIPHON

But no. Death cannot be the only end of it.
In the silent interstices he thinks at times
he hears her, a voice less insistent

than it was in life, a voice more patient,
with all the time now in the world to wait
for her distracted son to look up from

whatever he is doing to begin to listen.
How often in the watches of the night, before
the birds are up, his wife of thirty years

asleep beside him, his sons long scattered,
he thinks he hears his mother in the lift
of windchimes. If she speaks to him, it is

with a voice familiar both and strange, without
the old accumulated weight of grievance, a voice
made clear by the distance each has traveled.

"Sì come rota ch'igualmente è mossa,"
the pilgrim wrote at journey's end. What one
yearns to do and what one must, one now, "like

a wheel revolving uniformly—by
the Love that moves the sun and other stars."
These are the words his rabbi gave him,

who reached through seven centuries
to blood them for him, turning them
from sounds which should have been

his birthright but were not, to syllables
on which to feed, and which his mother
gave him first, who mingled tears in with

the milk she fed him, tears for her own fall,
and then for his. Nothing for it then
but to find his way to mass in the village

north of here, and kneel before the tiny altar
off to the side, and light a candle there
which will burn among the others, small wheels

of fire that tug against their wicks, as if
eager now to join the great wheel that is
the morning sun come up to greet them.

NOTES

"Shadow Portrait": Just days before he took his own life, Hart Crane, believing he had failed as a poet, took a razor and slashed to ribbons the portrait with down casteyes which the Mexican painter, David Siquieros, had done of him the year before.

"Ghost": Cf. *The Aeneid, Bk. II,* 282 ff., in which two serpents entwine themselves about Laocoön's two sons, before turning on the father himself.

"The Statue": A public statue of Publius Ovidius Naso, which stands in the main square of his native town high in the Abruzzi mountains.

"Quid Pro Quo": CHENANGO VALLEY: site of Colgate University. CONFESSIONS: St. Augustine's autobiography. SUMMA: St. Thomas Aquinas's *Summa Theologica.* TRACTATE: The reference is to the *Tractatus* of Ludwig Wittgenstein. VANNI FUCCI'S FIGS: The "fig" is an obscene gesture made with the thumb jutting through the index and middle fingers of the clenched fist. Cf. Dante's *Inferno,* the close of Canto XXIV and the opening of XXV, which begins with the gesture which will bring on the Pistoian the wrath of serpents much like those that crushed Laocoön centuries before. The translation is mine:

> Al fine de le sue parole il ladro
> le mani alzò con amendue le fiche,
> gridando: "Togli, Dio, ch'a te le squadro!"

> When he had finished, the thief made figs
> of both his fists, and raising them, cried,
> "Take that, God, these are both for you!"

"Then": BETA SIGMA: A now defunct fraternity at Manhattan College which may well have served as the original for the one portrayed in the film *Animal House.*

"The Republic": The unnamed police officer here is Frank Serpico, my student in Humanities 201, which I taught at the John Jay College of Criminal Justice when classes were held at the Police Academy on East 23rd Street. Serpico was an extraordinarily courageous cop who blew the whistle on corruption in the New York City Police Department in the late 1960s. Some may remember Peter Maas's *Serpico*, and Al Pacino in the film of that name. The names of the other officers—many of whom I still have fond memories of—have been changed.

"One Dark Night": The poem is a translation of St. John of the Cross's "Noche Oscura," which the sixteenth-century Spanish mystic wrote while in prison.

"And This Thy Harbor": THIS WATER FLOWS EAST: Cf. Ezekiel, Ch. 47, in the Jerusalem Bible translation. MESHED STEEL CABLES: Cf. the proem to Hart Crane's *The Bridge*. ST. DISMAS: Or Dysmas, one of the names offered by tradition for the nameless thief crucified alongside Jesus, to whom in Luke's account Jesus promised paradise.

"Antiphon": SÌ COME ROTA . . . : Cf. the final lines of the final canto of Dante's *Paradiso*, and Allen Mandelbaum's translation:

> *A l'alta fantasia qui mancò possa;*
> *ma già volgeva il mio disio e'l velle,*
> *sì come rota ch'igualmente è mossa,*
> *l'amor che move il sole e l'altre stelle.*

> *Here force failed my high fantasy; but my*
> *desire and will were moved already—like*
> *a wheel revolving uniformly—by*
> *the Love that moves the sun and other stars.*

Paul Mariani was born in New York City in 1940, and has lived most of his life on Long Island and later in western Massachusetts with his wife and three sons. He is the author of four other poetry collections: *Timing Devices* (1979), *Crossing Cocytus* (1982), *Prime Mover* (1985), and *Salvage Operations: New & Selected Poems* (1990). He is also the author of commentaries on Hopkins and on Williams, and a collection of essays on modern and contemporary poetry, as well as acclaimed biographies of John Berryman, Robert Lowell, and William Carlos Williams, for which he was named a finalist for an American Book Award. Among other awards he has received NEA, NEH, and Guggenheim Fellowships. He is Distinguished University Professor at the University of Massachusetts/Amherst, where he has taught for the past twenty-five years.